D1571556

DENISE RILEY

Dry Air

Published by VIRAGO PRESS Limited 1985
41 William IV Street, London WC2N 4DB

Copyright © Denise Riley 1985

British Library Cataloguing in Publication Data
Riley, Denise
   Dry air.
   I. Title
   821'.914   PS3568.I377/

  ISBN 0-86068-539-X

Printed in Great Britain by
Anchor-Brendon, Tiptree, Essex
Photoset by Rowland Phototypesetting Ltd
Bury St Edmunds, Suffolk

Some of these poems have previously appeared in *Grosseteste Review*,
In'hui, *Perfect Bound*, *Feminist Review*, and in the author's earlier books;
Marxism for Infants (Street Editions, 1977), *No Fee* (with Wendy
Mulford) (Street Editions, 1978), *Some Poems 1968–1978* (with Wendy
Mulford) (CMR Press, 1982), and *Living a Life*.

Contents

From *Marxism for Infants*
A note on sex and 'the reclaiming of language'   7
Making a Liberty Belle   8
she's imagining her wife . . .   9
postcard . . .   10
she has ingested her wife . . .   11
There's nothing for it . . .   12
I heard the water . . .   13
I lived with my children . . .   14
An infant   15
it's november . . .   16
You have a family? . . .   17
hold fast in arms . . .   18
such face bones . . .   19
assume a country . . .   20

From *No Fee*
In 1970   23
A Nueva York   24
Affections must not   26
Work   28
To the islands   29
And you knew it   30
Not what you think   31

Versions of six poems by Friedrich Hölderlin (1770–1843)
The middle of life   35
Taking leave   36
The ages   37
If on the far side . . .   38

Each day I take . . .   40
Home   41

The man of grass   43
History   43
Our youth and mine   44
Mastering the art of English art   46
No, not enough   46
Lost in Europe   47
Ah, so   48
To the lakes   48
Got to get back   49
What I do   50
No   51
To the fields   52
The ambition to advise speaks   53
The ambition to not be particular speaks   54
The ambition to not be resentful speaks   55
Two ambitions to remember   56
The Cloud Rose   57
How short   58
Song   59
No work in Britain; working abroad   60
To the city   62
In Granada, 1936   63

From Marxism for Infants

A note on sex and 'the reclaiming of language'

The Savage is flying back home from the New Country
in native-style dress with a baggage of sensibility
to gaze on the ancestral plains with the myths thought up
and dreamed in her kitchens as guides

                                        She will be discovered
as meaning is flocking densely around the words seeking a way
any way in between the gaps, like a fertilisation

                                        The work is
e.g. to write 'she' and for that to be a statement
of fact only and not a strong image
of everything which is not-you, which sees you

The new land is colonised, though its prospects are empty

The Savage weeps as landing at the airport
she is asked to buy wood carvings, which represent herself

Making a Liberty Belle

my exercise book of twenty
years ago says neatly, I guess
copied out of an Annual
'to make a Liberty Belle
White Ballet
Skirt with a
Layer of Blue Net
Dotted with
Silver Stars.
Back and Front
Panels Red White
Striped Cotton.
Tie Bandolier of White Stuff
Over One Shoulder
and under opposite, write
word "LIBERTY" in Indian
Ink.   Cut headdress from
Gold or painted paper
Cornet of same
with screw of
orangey-red paper inside
to represent the Flame'

she's imagining her wife & how will she live her?   when
the wife goes off to endless meetings in the rain
she'll say aah I admire her spirit bravo la petite
& when her belly swells into an improbable curve
the she-husband will think Yes, it was me who caused that,
and more generously, Biology, you are wonderful

postcard;   'I live in silence here
a wet winter   the baby's well
I give her bear's names   Ursula
Mischa   Pola   Living alone makes
anyone crazy, especially with children'

I live in silence here

the tongue as a swan's neck
full and heavy in the mouth

speech as a sexed thing

the speaking limb is stilled

she has ingested her wife
she has re-inhabited her own wrists
she is squatting in her own temples, the
fall of light on hair or any decoration
is re-possessed.   'She' is I.

There's nothing for it   Your 'father' and I
Biologically, a lack.   The child tries manfully
He calls it special seed but he gets confused at
                                                    school

An unselfconscious wife is raised high as a flag over
                the playground and burns up

I heard the water freezing in a thousand launderettes
with a dense white shudder
I heard the roar of a thousand vacuum cleaners
stammer away into uncarpeted silence

today it is all grandiose domestic visions truly

in St Petersburg now Leningrad we have communal kitchens
the cooking is dreadful but we get to meet our friends

I lived with my children in a warm bright and
harmonious room which formed the crest of a high
timber scaffolding – a room on stilts.   Outside
it was a black night, an old railway yard,
abandoned tracks, a high wind.   Our room
although too small for our needs was glowing and
secure despite the fact that it had no roof,
that its walls led straight upwards to the
black clear sky.
        I left there briefly and encountered x
who pointed upwards to show where we should both
go.   A smooth platform hung in the sky, its
only access a long swaying cord joined to its
midpoint, the end of which drifted against my
face.   It looked impossible but I was not
disheartened.

An infant

who lives in 'feminism' like a warm square
who composes 'pushes hair back wearily' on a bicycle
who has always been older than twenty-eight and is
                              half-killed in oldness
who doubts daily and is silly for something or other

who comes in the shut house where she is

whose face is floating in its still sleep skin
whose face is features under clear water
whose days come bursting purely to her surface

who is watched asleep in a hawk's heart
who is hovered over in a passion
who is new enough not to mind that
who is perfectly right enough to be generous

whose fingers have a fresh will
whose face is all its future

it's november child and time goes
in little bursts   a warm room
clean and squeaky as an orange pip
in a wet landscape

You have a family?   It is impermissible.

There is only myself   complete and arched
like a rainbow or an old tree
with gracious arms descending
over the rest of me who is the young
children in my shelter who grow
up under my leaves and rain
In our own shade
we embrace each other gravely &
look out tenderly upon the world

seeking only contemporaries
and speech and light, no father.

hold fast in arms before astonished eyes
whom you must grasp throughout great changes
constant and receptive as a capital city

is now a fire   now a frozen hand
a rainstorm   white birds
a rotting log   a young boy
a savaged sheep   an indifference

a kind of seriousness,   a kind of rage

and through each transforming
yourself to be not here whose
body shapes a hundred lights a
glowing strip of absence night's
noisy and particular who
vanishes with that flawless sense
of occasion I guess you'd have if
only I knew you at first light
leaving 'the wrong body', old, known

such face bones honeycombed sockets
of strained eyes outlined in warm

light aching wrapped in impermeable
coating of pleasure going off wild

on the light-headed train   'will write
& write what there is beyond anything'

it is the 'spirit' burns in &
through 'sex' which we know about

saying It's true, I won't place or
describe it   It *is* & refuses the law

assume a country
held by small walls

assume a landscape
with lakes & the need for protection

assume a house
with shut doors and a fire

the house in the landscape
which roads irradiate

the hand that rocks the cradle
erect at every crossroads

*

not liking as mirrored
but likeness, activity

a whole life for likeness
after the silence

and does try and will try
and the past weight and the future

From No Fee

the houses are murmuring with many small pockets of emotion
on which spongy ground adults' lives are being erected & paid
                                                    for daily
while their feet and their children's feet are tangled around
                                        like those of fen larks
in the fine steely wires which run to & fro between love &
                        economics

affections must not support the rent

I.   neglect.   the.   house

Work

For a time self-evident light all tremendously clear
to be sat down under in abstract triumph, still shaking with
luck and nearly-wasn't; later in a flood of in this case loosestrife
dead wood dead children billowing in moondaisies set to
piped music tears and dreadful violence, only tolerable years
                                                    later
through aesthetics to make red noons of what was at the time real
                                                    blood.
So it goes on asserting the unbearable solid detail as real work,
                                                    Lissitsky;
'work must be accepted
as one of the functions of the living organism
in the same way as the beating of the heart
or the activity of the nerve centres
so that it will be afforded the same protection'
and no sleep pricks out clear and small
people in landscapes who are pushing up around the sides of
                                                    larger
things. Dear attention; fix that point precisely where
landscapes first got peopled & painting set off on a series of
                                                    humane
journeys south to venice; so for saints to be warming their hands
                                                    at lions
on khaki mountains, netted camels to be arching home midfield,
black light and cliffs of rain to be taking their time across
                                                    horizons
and an evil to heave itself out of a brown pond, foreground,
                                                    unobserved.
Look out, saint. Not to be your own passions' heroine
else, invented, you'll stick in them. So, telegram: forget.

To the islands

I hear all sounds within my ear

I passed them mowing
we were dragging uphill

a voyage.   the ship's bar
two women come in, & break their silence

take two my head is a chance
that place is cold it has no children

I hear all sounds within my ear

it is on white sand one morning
nothing to be said, the silk sea

in the evening it is floating weed islands
black against a light and a water
these are either blue or they are gold

writing politics is a luscious glow
and gives a quick buzz to your style

And you knew it

what are these airs?
& all fair-headed grass

mournful, ironic, gestural, moral
you can radiate everything you are

all words return to bright

heavy echoes run in me

*

if the sky moves so
indigo down to dragged plane wastes
but through such blues
                              True in time for
then time measure
if the light fade
then the light fade

*

as the quick dawn fly
the smart head turn
I know

as the slow movement out
as the gradual light break

Not what you think

wonderful light
viridian summers
deft boys
no thanks

Versions of six poems by
Friedrich Hölderlin (1770–1843)

The middle of life

With yellow pears
& all wild roses
land hangs on the lake.
Amorous swans dip
heads in
sober water.

Where, when winter
comes, will I
find flowers, where
sun and shadows
of the earth?
Walls stand
speechless & cold
in the wind
weathercocks rattle.

('Halfte des Lebens', *written between 1802 and 1806*)

Taking leave

I've cut into
your golden rest
often enough; you
know things from me
you could well have done
without – dark griefs.

Forget them. Forgive.
Clouds
lift off the quiet moon;
so you, dear light,
gleam steadily.

('Die Abbitte', *written between 1796 and 1798*)

The ages

You towns of Euphrates!
You streets of Palmyra!
You forests of pillars
in wastes of the plain
what are you? You passed
beyond breathing, your crowns
snatched by smoke, by
divinity's flame.
Now I sit under clouds
each has its own peace
under well-arranged oaks
on the heath of the deer
and strange and dead to me
the souls of the blest.

('Lebensalter', *written between 1799 and 1806*)

If on the far side . . .

If on the far side of all this
you who shared my grief
could still know me
the past might prove some good.

How do you think your love waits?
in gardens where after hard
and obscure years we found each other?
Now by the river of the first world

I must admit there was something
to be said for your look
when you turned round cheerfully that once,
you shut-away man with your

dark face. How the hours ran on
and struck my spirit with the truth
of how badly it had been cut off. I
understood then, I was with you.

And now you want to bring everything
back to me again, get it in
writing – I too am compelled
to say everything about what was;

those times, birds, trees, bright paths,
low scrub, the sand we walked on and small
flowers. The house, walls
green with ivy and

the greenish dark of tall avenues.
Nights and mornings
we were there, we talked
looked at each other.

The boy came alive in my arms.
He'd come, heart broken, from
those fields he'd sadly sent me to.

but he kept hold of the names
of rare places, he remembered
what flowered by the shore, things
I'd cared for in my country.

They are hidden things
you only see from a high point
where you overlook the sea
though no-one wants to be down there.

Think about her; she was glad
that dazzling day
which started with touches and stories.
They were fine days.
A terrible dusk followed them.

You are so all alone in the lovely world,
my love, as you insist on telling me
– but then you don't exactly know that . . .

('Wenn aus der Ferne', *written after 1806*)

Like streams, the end of something rushes me away
It spreads itself out like Asia.

(Fragment, after 1806)

Each day I take . . .

Each day I take a different path
now to the river, now the wood
or to the rocks where roses are

I climb the hill where I look out
but find you nowhere in the light

my beauty, and my words are gone
into the air. Our words were right.

Yes, you are far away; your face
and clear sounds of your life are lost.
Where are the songs that brought me peace?
This man's grown old; the earth lacks grace.

Go well. Each day my restless mind
goes out to you, is turned away.
My eyes strain after you to see
lightly straight through to where you stay.

('Wohl geh' ich täglich', *written between 1798 and 1800*)

Home

Happy the sailor, home to his still river
from far-off islands where he's worked.
I would like a home to reach
though what but sadness have I earned?

You river banks, you brought me up;
now can you calm the hurts of love?
Woods of my childhood, will you give
me peace of mind if I return?

('Die Heimat', *written between 1796 and 1798*)

The man of grass

on water mountains glacial days
o marriage springs the romps the interviews
pale walls of gold surmount the vetch

it is not right when posing moons
elaborate the heart's desire
in quelling syllables dried like rushes
that we are not chinese that we don't want to be

History

can we revolt to con the man
the idiot taurus won't let be

the candour of the marzipan
hermaphrodité's silvery ways

night took us by surprise
sparkling slowly with tears

Our youth and mine

Can years and years of folding in to the rumoured heart of / be
    in vain? as each
you repeats *you* in a clearer light, more amazed untiring openings
in the shine of this-face-only, the long astonished soft whistle
at speech known, can the most elaborate
swing out at last into a flat lit day? say it could –
a tortuous road, that, to go down & back to here, like one of
    those zen riddles
you can guess the end of anyway –
love looked-for & returning like rain
& as randomly dispersed to a thousand equally radiant faces
as broad and unparticular as grass.
No time or characters in being happy, but each fresh angel's
the split image of that guest you'd long forgotten, & would have
    sworn was not

& still the immediate travelling problem, that there really *is*
    separation, geography,
& gets no younger (so wearing out in place I don't look up
but hear the sky raked by fortunates who are going away)
with you in the town of x where myself arrives
a good day later than my body on the train
while my imagination's entertained itself a whole week in
    advance
but at the last moment fights shy of getting incorporated –
how then ever to coincide? but sometimes it *does* work,
namelessly, and that's alive as can be.

Who ageing through local acts peopled by the persons of the
    drama
is fixed at the sites of institutionalised pain,
of which yes, you can have as much as you like
you can remember everything said that killed you, you are word-
    perfect
28 years of rehearsing got it off by heart for you
you examine it each night lovingly where it is all yours all for always
and it is a bright animal that rises in your sleep
each morning it swims neat as an eel between the wet dishes
small face, it will pick you out at the playground gates
or you could take it out with you to meetings, there are crowds
and you can become their violence with an easy permission

and here is the Madonna, she is professionally sad
she has had her day which has quite done for her, the Child
is separate and smiles. And this spreadeagled woman here
is not merely outlined in knives, but has in fact been pierced and
    has died of that.

Everything you think meets and rushes forward from many
    different directions
loudly all at once in a glow and a shout, knee-deep in pound
    notes.

Mastering the art of English art

In the gardens of the Villa Doria Pamphili
it's about this and about that:
more and more blue, those classical ladies,
looking like rain, the Fiats go streaming
                              over the bridge.

No, not enough

Not enough sleep again
narrows your eyes.
Oh thirty-three.

Lost in Europe

One evening in a London fog
a type approximating to
my lover came to meet me and
the sort of look that he gave me
it made me hang my head in shame

You refer my name and place
a million bodies brought in daily
live unity no name no face
my heart has left my history
so goodbye form I feel no more
I want for myself in this space
a name quite free of memory

As the threshold is heavy with grain
the hand army starts counting. If
you understand shortage
against full fields, if you know lack
against wide furrows, great crops are there.
The hand army waves over them.

(The first stanza is a version of the start of a poem by Guillaume Apollinaire, the second uses some lines by Catherine Pozzi)

Ah, so

Speaking apart, I hear my voice run on
in the red heart of an ear, an ear coils round me
disturb the text; you don't disturb the world

This train is inserted across England, its country
get a sense of history   of history

I found some change in my trouser pocket, like
                                a man

To the lakes

likeness looks back at you with serious eyes
so you can bear to be looked at too

a different speaker shows you how
at night it is calmer than we thought

difference has raced away into the texts
there let it weep I'll none of it for now

but rejoice to hold steady
in a grey blue light

Got to get back

Is your proud desire
emotion would not expire
that it not tire
liar

'the air was so thick with gender
you could have cut it with a knife'
ouch, in a melancholy dream of truth

Is this love
changes?   Birds
circle.   Miaow, miaow.

You rising a snowstorm and falling
and settling in the hollows of everything

below the boats are waiting, drawn up with a long low laugh
and Georgia is there, its tall white fields

You are just stunned
by others, who they are

What I do

An even time
all to myself, though
lately it hasn't been,
more violent. My
death still will
skip on, 'This way,
my love', I know
but privately
I cross my heart; that
shakes, though, the noise-maker.
I am in several cupboards
deep, and wish well out,
wish out from this
dark air of china.
Is my name 'skeleton'
or only 'cup'?
A crack of light falls round me.

No

All the towels are red
the navy towel and the black
blood-soaked
and the white dress has slipped
to the bloodied floor.

This one you lose you could not love.
You were deceived, your flat blood knew
to open its bright factual eye.
This that you leak you never grew.

The officer is at the scarlet door.
Here is his evidence. Some body lied.
That body's mine but I am it.
And I am it and I have lied.

To the fields

Walking on grass
my friend ahead, I
behind with
the child. She
couldn't keep up
and wouldn't. The light
drained everything of
colour, the cattle
and pale daisies. I
didn't know his
mind then. By
evening, families
strung out across
the fields for
cars and homes
or we too

The ambition to advise speaks

'Do not be charmed by the long arch of your own trajectory
but shoot along boldly on the hard gaze of the straight

put yourself on the margins but don't be endlessly naming them
be taken with yourself if you are but keep quiet about it
& choose yourself a gender but be prepared to be flexible here

clear colour will be a help in this
say no to sociology always
in any event you will need music

remembering not to think yourself happy until you are
                              which you will know
then go for it'

The ambition to not be particular speaks

'I cannot tell what gives each voice its tune –
some furious tenderness of buried words
or interference from the streets
and their hazardous crying –

but if for me some words must be exhumed
out of their sunken heat they must be cooled
to the grace of being common –

so to achieve my great colourlessness
I dive into the broken brilliant world
and float in it unindividuated, whitely'

The ambition to not be resentful speaks

'No-one drinks to speak out wildly
against the coils of the snake regret
no-one is troubled for mirrors
of greenish foxed glass

No-one has mislaid her children
or never met her mother and father
everyone has clean limbs unveined
and runs lightly on the dollar

Everyone has an upright husband
and something to call loudly on the sidewalk
a few are even beautiful
which is the last annoyance

Let the sun rush in me
like a tree of scarlet leaves
that I may not be so gracelessly
dark with a conceit of strangeness'

Two ambitions to remember

A.   The shapes of faces stiff with joy
     stir in my mind but do not speak.

B.   The drive out of town
     the fans of pale branches

A.   I see my deafened future come
     while those true words that have no mouth
     and leap and dazzle silently
     go streaming down the fiery air.

B.   The crush of trees' thin
     limbs inward and inward

A.   Some words you may use only once.
     Repeat them to some newer heart
     and all your accuracy is gone.

B.   To sail into the lit tunnel
     a rush of orange, quietly

A.   Is happiness this anxious then?
     I know that I will be outraged
     when at my death I won't recall
     each detailed tenderness of speech.

B.   A square of sun
     slides on the roughened wall

A.   Insane with loneliness I wring
     the tissues of the air to force
     the full words that would answer me.

56

The Cloud Rose

The house had its teeth in her leg.
Her sorrow had made a cloud rose
and the cloud rose encompassed them.
Soon she became it though it was her end.
Old mauves fogged the stairs while crimsons
sunk in dark corners and streaked them
with vaporous skin petals. Cream and scarlet
they massed hesitant in every drawer.
Papers blurred. The child ate petals.

*

A cloud rose on the horizon of the morning
with a plume like the breath of a whale at sea
It was the cloud rose whose heavy dew
had watered the documents into the earth
and the flat men and her fingers fallen to rain

In rain-divided air to rise
to what she may, and is not said to, be

In the air a shadow of a child circled attentively
in the cloudless air
in the unimaged air
in that dry air of no flower I long to breathe

How short

I pull clouds away from my eyebrows
and my mist hair parts before my face.
A voice of rock, fine powder.

Words fly into my head
in bed as if they must be said.

A wind
races the dry grass by the tarmac.
White rubbish.

Is there no vividness
will shake despair.
Or lie down to it, longing.

Song

A high and brilliant
arc streaks over the
dark plains to
see, its arrow
gaze shoots
generously beyond death.

Above the explosive dark
its eyes trail a hot dew

of love. A knife parts
this way & that through
bruised clouds, it
hangs freshly wet.

*

A fine fold
beyond the thickening hooks

A pale strain
under the matted sounds

A faint glitter
behind the rough stuff of dark mesh
of lily light / drag me through

No business dying.

No work in Britain; working abroad

A piece of sky scratches my bare leg.
It is bright blue chicory flowers
angled down the school road.
Now in my homeland they are all asleep.

*

Where have you got to?
This is all extraordinary.

I'm private
here, & write by the window.

Bedroom clouds.
Azaleas. Objects.
Different days.

*

The hot singing forests
and the air of democracy.
Lost men at the gates. Black
sharp shrubs and eucalypts
on the sweet plateaux are
shining in waves.

*

Glacial blue gleam
cliffs. Sonorous water
off Charing Cross Bridge and
then lift your eyes.

How many towns
I lean across, wandering.

*

Red fields, red soil
or tawny soil.
Small trees like gum
trees run through soft light.
There is all day, all
day to go.

*

The sea springs from the marsh
in a violet wedge.

A fine black gauze
veils the sky over
before your eyes.

*

Some trees
and a corner of the institution.

Where are dark cities, friends,
my native daughter.

To the city

New jumps ahead
a running lilt
adventurers to
burning horizons
It is this sight, a future
        that we hold

who noisily softly sleep
as dying fires

as Albion Rd patience
now grazes the flaring
clouds yellow
and high flats

you seven beauties
sing
to not die down

In Granada, 1936

Eyeless, the dark flower
must marry the wall.
Stone gold overflows
authority's gesture.
Swimmer, reply: skull, reply.

This light's
great broken leaves.
This arch of blood.
A music, waiting.